W0246989

Kahlil Gibran (1883–1931) was a Lebanese-American writer, poet and artist, best known for his masterpiece *The Prophet*. A visionary thinker, Gibran's works explore themes of love, freedom, purpose and the human spirit, blending profound simplicity with universal truths that resonate across cultures and generations. His poetic prose and philosophical insights have made *The Prophet* one of the most beloved books of all time, inspiring millions with its timeless wisdom.

Gill Hasson has 20 years' experience teaching and writing on a range of issues to do with personal and professional development, mental health and wellbeing. She is the author of more than 22 books: the bestselling *Mindfulness*, *Mindfulness Pocketbook*, *Emotional Intelligence*, *Positive Thinking*, the *Sunday Times* bestseller *How to Deal with Difficult People*, plus other books on the subjects of resilience, communication skills and assertiveness.

THE PROPHET

ALSO IN THE SERIES

The Art of War
Autobiography of a Yogi
Meditations
Think and Grow Rich

THE PROPHET

Timeless Wisdom Distilled

KAHLIL GIBRAN

Edited by Gill Hasson

First published in Great Britain by John Murray One in 2025
An imprint of John Murray Press

SRD

The material for *The Prophet* is based on the 1923 edition, published by Alfred A. Knopf, New York, and is now in the public domain. This edition is not sponsored or endorsed by, or otherwise affiliated with Kahlil Gabran, his families or heirs. Images from Project Gutenberg. The illustrations in this book are reproduced from original drawings by the author.

A CIP catalogue record for this title is available from the British Library

Hardback ISBN 978 1 399 82154 4
ebook ISBN 978 1 399 82155 1

Typeset by KnowledgeWorks Global Ltd.

Printed and bound in India by Manipal Technologies Limited, Manipal

John Murray Press policy is to use papers that are natural, renewable and recyclable products and made from wood grown in sustainable forests. The logging and manufacturing processes are expected to conform to the environmental regulations of the country of origin.

John Murray Press
Carmelite House
50 Victoria Embankment
London EC4Y 0DZ

John Murray Press
123 S. Broad St., Ste 2750
Philadelphia, PA 19109

www.johnmurraypress.co.uk

John Murray Press, part of Hodder & Stoughton Limited
An Hachette UK company

Contents

Preface

ORIGINALLY PUBLISHED IN 1923, *The Prophet* by the Lebanese-American writer Kahlil Gibran (1883–1931) tells the story of the prophet Almustafa (Arabic for "the chosen one") who, after 12 years living in the mythical city of Orphalese, is about to voyage home. As he waits at the harbour for his ship to berth, the people of the city gather at the dockside. Realizing this is the last opportunity they will have to benefit from his wisdom and advice, one person after another asks the prophet to speak on a different issue.

> And he and the people proceeded towards the great square before the temple.
>
> And there came out of the sanctuary a woman whose name was Almitra. And she was a seeress.
>
> And he looked upon her with exceeding tenderness, for it was she who had first sought and believed in him when he had been but a day in their city. And she hailed him, saying:
>
> "Prophet of God, in quest of the uttermost, long have you searched the distances for your ship.
>
> "And now your ship has come, and you must needs go.
>
> "Deep is your longing for the land of your memories and the dwelling place of your greater desires; and our love would not bind you nor our needs hold you.
>
> "Yet this we ask ere you leave us, that you speak to us and give us of your truth.

"And we will give it unto our children, and they unto their children, and it shall not perish.

"In your aloneness you have watched with our days, and in your wakefulness you have listened to the weeping and the laughter of our sleep.

"Now therefore disclose us to ourselves, and tell us all that has been shown you of that which is between birth and death." ("On the Coming of the Ship")

Almustafa agrees, and the first subject he speaks of is love – the foundation of many of the other issues he is asked about. He emphasizes the power of love to bring joy and fulfilment, as well as the pain and challenges that can come with love. He says that a prerequisite of love is freedom; that love is not possessive, that it should be given freely with no expectation of anything in return. It is a message which is further reflected in the part love plays in marriage and having children.

Figures of speech

The prophet often talks of the issues under discussion in terms of duality and paradox – of each having two aspects that, although they have opposing meanings, are also dependent on one another. He explains that the answer to many issues lies in the relationship and interaction of two forces. He also emphasizes that balance is important – one aspect is no bigger or stronger than the other, but integral to the whole. Examples he speaks of include giving and receiving, reason and passion, good and evil, joy and sorrow, life and death: "For life and death are one."

The Prophet is written as a prose poem and uses many of the traditional devices of poetry. The use of metaphor – the indirect comparison of two things by stating that one thing is another thing – is a notable feature of *The Prophet*. For example, in Almustafa's statement "Your pain is the breaking of the shell that encloses your understanding" ("On Pain"), he is comparing emotional pain to the breaking open of a shell that contains a realization, an understanding of a truth. Another way he makes comparisons is with the use of simile – that is, by making an explicit comparison: "The just from the unjust [...] they stand together before the face of the sun even as the black thread and the white are woven together" ("On Crime and Punishment").

Other literary and poetic devices Gibran uses are aphorisms (short statements expressing a truth), such as "Alone and without his nest shall the eagle fly across the sun", and personification (the attribution of human characteristics to animals or features of the natural world): "What of the old serpent who cannot shed his skin, and calls all others naked and shameless?" ("On Law").

Spirituality

The theme of spirituality recurs throughout *The Prophet* and is influenced by the rich traditions of Christianity, Islam (especially Sufism) and the Bahá'í Faith as well as by American Transcendentalism (Gibran himself was raised as a Maronite Christian). Many of the people who ask the prophet to speak understand the practical purpose of the subjects they ask about but are unaware of the spiritual aspects.

The ploughman, for example, asks the prophet to talk about work. The ploughman knows of the physical nature of work but is unaware of its spiritual aspect, and so the prophet explains how honour and love are integral to the work we do.

Likewise, the innkeeper, who asks about eating and drinking, is used to preparing and serving food and drink for his guests, yet he hasn't considered that, like the animals and plants we eat, we are all part of the natural world – part of a continual cycle of life and death. And in answer to a request from the astronomer, the prophet explains the eternal, immeasurable nature of time and the timelessness of life.

Romanticism

The influence of Romanticism in *The Prophet* reflects the author Kahlil Gibran's idealistic approach to life. Romanticism – an artistic and intellectual movement that originated in Europe in the late 18th and early 19th centuries – championed the subjective – the spontaneity of emotions and feelings – over the objective – measured reason and logic. (It should be noted, however, that in "On Reason and Passion", Gibran departs from the Romantic rejection of rationalism and instead acknowledges reason as a necessary balance to and support for feelings and emotions.)

Romanticism rejected the adherence to form, structure and order proposed by the Age of Enlightenment, an intellectual, scientific and philosophical movement that occurred in Europe in the 17th and the 18th centuries. Instead, Romanticism emphasized individuality, creativity, imagination, the spontaneous, an appreciation of nature and beauty, the transcendental and the supernatural.

About this book

More than one hundred years after it was first published, Kahlil Gibran's *The Prophet* remains a classic of spiritual literature that offers readers an insight into the paradoxes of human existence, its unique blend of poetry and philosophy encouraging us to find answers, meaning and purpose in our own life.

This book, *The Prophet: Timeless Wisdom Distilled* by Kahlil Gibran, does not claim to offer a definitive interpretation of *The Prophet* – it is simply *one* interpretation, *my* interpretation of selected writings from the book. As Almustafa himself says when speaking about self-knowledge:

> Say not, "I have found the truth," but rather, "I have found *a* truth."
>
> Say not, "I have found the path of the soul." Say rather, "I have met the soul walking upon my path." ("On Self-Knowledge")

On each left-hand page you will read a passage from one of the subjects that the prophet speaks of. On each facing page is an interpretation of his words and, occasionally, further advice on how you might make use of the prophet's advice in your own life.

ON LOVE

“ Then said Almitra, Speak to us of Love.

And he raised his head and looked upon the people, and there fell a stillness upon them. And with a great voice he said: ”

"When love beckons to you,
follow him,
Though his ways are hard
and steep.
And when his wings enfold you
yield to him,
Though the sword hidden among
his pinions may wound you."

LOVE IS NOT something you choose; it's something that chooses you. And when it does, surrender to love, follow love, even though loving can be hard – a steep learning curve.

As a winged entity, like an angel or a bird, love can lift you to great heights, but you are also vulnerable – susceptible to being hurt; the sword hidden in love's feathers can wound you.

“For even as love crowns you so shall he crucify you. Even as he is for your growth so is he for your pruning.”

Even though love can bring you to the highest, most perfect state of being, it can torment and torture you. It can leave you vulnerable and exposed.

As much as love allows you to grow, love also acts to prune you – remove all that is unnecessary or undesirable – and reshape you to make you the best version of yourself. Just as a plant must be cut back so that it might grow more healthy, your old habits, selfish instincts and limiting beliefs will be challenged and checked by the experience of loving and being loved.

" Like sheaves of corn he gathers
you unto himself.
He threshes you to make you
naked.
He sifts you to free you from your
husks.
He grinds you to whiteness.
He kneads you until you are pliant;
And then he assigns you to his
sacred fire, that you may become
sacred bread for God's
sacred feast. "

LOVE STRIPS EVERYTHING from you and leaves you pure – free from all that's irrelevant. In this way, you can be reformed/transformed into something humbler than yourself, and yet, like dough that has been left to prove and rise, become something more than yourself.

" But if in your fear you would
seek only love's peace and
love's pleasure,
Then it is better for you that you
cover your nakedness and pass out
of love's threshing-floor,
Into the seasonless world where
you shall laugh, but not all of your
laughter, and weep, but not all of
your tears. "

IF YOU DON'T want to open yourself up and you wish love to only give you peace and pleasure, you must take your leave of it, for it cannot be embraced timidly without consequence.

Without love you may still experience pain and happiness, but you will not feel pain in its fullness and you will not experience complete happiness.

Without committing to the full experience of love, we may as well leave the place where love does its real work – the threshing-floor, where grain is separated from chaff.

You will still experience pain and happiness, but you will not feel pain in its fulness and you will not experience complete happiness.

“ Love gives naught but itself and
takes naught but from itself.
Love possesses not nor would it
be possessed;
For love is sufficient unto love. ”

Love is complete – it needs nothing and takes nothing. It is not a contract and does not imply ownership, nor wish to be controlled. It takes only from itself – in other words, it draws on its own abundance. *The Prophet*'s radical view of love unhooks it from ego or transaction.

" And think not you can direct the course of love, for love, if it finds you worthy, directs your course. "

DON'T THINK YOU can choose what path love will take, when and how love will appear and progress. It is not a vehicle that you steer, obedient to your hopes and plans. Instead – if love chooses you – trust that it will guide you on your path. If you surrender yourself to it, it will guide you to new and profound places.

“But if you love and must needs
have desires, let these be
your desires:
To melt and be like a running
brook that sings its melody to the
night. To know the pain of too
much tenderness.
To be wounded by your own
understanding of love;
And to bleed willingly and joyfully.
To wake at dawn with a winged
heart and give thanks for another
day of loving […].”

BUT IF YOU do love and you want anything from love, let it be this – to give your all and not hold back. And to understand and accept the pain of love and affection and to begin each day with gratitude for the opportunity to love.

ON MARRIAGE

“ Then Almitra spoke again and said, And what of Marriage, master? And he answered saying: ”

“You were born together, and together you shall be forevermore. You shall be together when the white wings of death scatter your days.”

On the day of your marriage, you are "born together"; together you have started something new that will last forever, even after you have both died, when "the white wings of death scatter your days".

Much as this sounds sentimental, this tender vision of marriage is deeply spiritual. He envisages marriage as the creation of a metaphysical bond that transcends time and space and lasts forever. Life may be fleeting, he suggests, but love is eternal.

“But let there be spaces in
your togetherness,
And let the winds of the heavens
dance between you.
Love one another, but make not a
bond of love:
Let it rather be a moving sea
between the shores of your souls.”

Marriage is a shared experience, but there needs to be a balance between time together and time apart. The spaces in marriage give it strength and allow each person to grow. Love one another, but don't let your love confine or constrict you – let it be free flowing.

“Fill each other’s cup but drink not
from one cup.
Give one another of your bread but
eat not from the same loaf. Sing
and dance together and be joyous,
but let each one of you be alone,
Even as the strings of a lute are
alone though they quiver with the
same music.
Give your hearts, but not into each
other’s keeping.”

SHARE WHAT YOU have with each other and contribute what you have to give. But don't be over reliant on each other; you're still individual people who exist beyond each other. Enjoy time together and enjoy time away from each other.

Give of your heart, but not to give it away completely. Instead, by each singing your own song, you can harmonize fruitfully.

In this way you can stay distinct, yet create beautiful music together.

"And stand together yet not too
near together:
For the pillars of the temple
stand apart,
And the oak tree and the cypress
grow not in each other's shadow."

JUST AS THE pillars of a temple stand apart – their strength and stability providing a force to support the roof – by standing "together yet not too near together" you support your marriage. Like a cypress and an oak tree, a person cannot grow in the shadow of another. Each must have room to stand in the sun and have a chance to shine.

ON CHILDREN

“ And a woman who held a babe against her bosom said, Speak to us of Children.
And he said: ”

“Your children are not your
children.
They are the sons and daughters
of Life’s longing for itself.
They come through you but not
from you,
And though they are with you yet
they belong not to you.”

In this quietly radical passage Gibran seeks to redefine the role of parent as steward and protector of a life passing through one's care. Your children are not your children. They are born from a greater power and are a manifestation of "life's longing for itself" – life's natural cycle and the need to continue existing. They come through you, are with you, but are individuals in their own right.

" You may give them your love but
not your thoughts,
For they have their own thoughts.
You may house their bodies but
not their souls,
For their souls dwell in the house
of tomorrow, which you cannot
visit, not even in your dreams.
You may strive to be like them, but
seek not to make them like you.
For life goes not backward nor
tarries with yesterday. "

LOVE YOUR CHILDREN and be there to guide them, but don't try to shape them in your own image. They'll have their own ideas, their own values and their own way of seeing the world – just as you did. A good parent will offer their child a safe place to grow, but their inner lives, their hopes and dreams, belong to a future you can't fully imagine.

Aim to have a strong connection with them, but don't expect them to follow your path or live your story. Life moves forward, not backward. They're not here to carry on your past – they're here to become themselves, in their own time and their own way.

Parenting is not about crafting replicas of ourselves, but about serving as custodians of possibility. This is both a challenge and a liberation: to love without seeking to control, and to lead without holding back another's path.

ON GIVING

"Then said a rich man, Speak
to us of Giving.
And he answered:"

“You give but little when you give of your possessions.
It is when you give of yourself that you truly give.”

GIVING MATERIAL THINGS is easy to do – it costs little of who you are. Real giving happens when you offer something deeper: your love, your time, your interest, your concern, encouragement and support, your knowledge and skills – that's when you really give.

> Opportunities for sharing and giving are often around you. Today, think of someone to whom you could give something of yourself. It could be to say hello, give a compliment or an invitation to dinner, or offer your help with something.

“For what are your possessions but
things you keep and guard for fear
you may need them tomorrow?
And what is fear of need but
need itself?
Is not dread of thirst when your
well is full, the thirst that
is unquenchable?”

So often, you hold on to your possessions in fear that, although you have no use for them now, you might need them at some point in the future. But fear of what you might need makes you needy.

As long as you think that you don't have enough, you won't have enough.

Free yourself from your fear of tomorrow's needs. Write a list of anything you own that you're holding on to just in case you need it in future. Next, write down where you could find, borrow or buy it again. Then you will know that, if you let something go but later find you need it, you will already have thought of what to do and where to get it again.

As the ancient Greek philosopher Socrates said: "The secret of happiness is not found in seeking more, but in developing the capacity to enjoy less."

"There are those who give little of the much which they have – and they give it for recognition and their hidden desire makes their gifts unwholesome.
And there are those who have little and give it all.
These are the believers in life and the bounty of life, and their coffer is never empty.
There are those who give with joy, and that joy is their reward.
And there are those who give with pain, and that pain is their baptism.
And there are those who give and know not pain in giving, nor do they seek joy, nor give with mindfulness of virtue;
They give as in yonder valley the myrtle breathes its fragrance into space."

THERE ARE THOSE who give little of what they have and so that others notice. However, these gifts are contaminated.

In contrast, there are people who have an abundance mindset. They may have a little but they are happy to share and to give what they have to others. They "give with joy, and that joy is their reward". They don't need anything in return.

And then there are those who simply give; it's neither difficult, joyful nor virtuous. Rather, it's in their nature, as natural as breathing, just as the myrtle – or any other sweet-perfumed flower – shares its fragrance freely with the world, without effort, pride or calculation.

" And is there aught you
would withhold?
All you have shall someday
be given;
Therefore give now, that the season
of giving may be yours and not
your inheritors'. "

WHAT IS IT that you are holding on to? Whatever it is, one day, it will all be possessed by someone else. You can't take it with you, so give now, while the choice is yours, not the choosing of those who come after you.

> It's better to give with a warm hand than a cold one.

“You often say, ‘I would give, but only to the deserving.’
[…]
Surely he who is worthy to receive his days and his nights, is worthy of all else from you.
And he who has deserved to drink from the ocean of life deserves to fill his cup from your little stream.”

IF YOU ONLY give to those who deserve it, how do you decide who deserves it? Anyone who deserves to be alive is worthy of receiving from others.

Know that, first, you have been given to. So, if you have deserved all that you have, then surely others deserve a share of that?

" And what desert greater shall there be, than that which lies in the courage and the confidence, nay the charity, of receiving?

[...]

And you receivers – and you are all receivers – assume no weight of gratitude, lest you lay a yoke upon yourself and upon him who gives. "

When it comes to receiving, know that it takes courage, confidence and dignity to believe yourself to be worthy of receiving.

To those that receive – and we are all receivers – don't feel uncomfortable or indebted, for discomfort and feeling indebted is a weight that pulls you both down.

> Giving and receiving are different aspects of the flow of the circulation upon which everything in nature, including ourselves, depends. If one aspect of this energy flow doesn't function, the circulation of energy becomes stuck, and the entire cycle ceases to function. Since we are also part of nature, we also need to both give and receive.
>
> Believe that you are just as deserving as anyone else of the good things in life. Be open to receiving and do so with grace.

ON EATING AND DRINKING

“Then an old man, a keeper of an inn, said, Speak to us of Eating and Drinking.

And he said:”

"Would that you could live on the fragrance of the earth, and like an air plant be sustained by the light. But since you must kill to eat, and rob the newly born of its mother's milk to quench your thirst, let it then be an act of worship."

WE CAN'T LIVE on light and air alone; we must kill to eat. But since killing is a violent act against a living thing, those who participate should do so with reverence – respect and appreciation – for the life that was taken to feed another life.

"When you kill a beast say to him
in your heart,
'By the same power that slays you,
I too am slain; and I too shall
be consumed. For the law that
delivered you into my hand shall
deliver me into a mightier hand.
Your blood and my blood is naught
but the sap that feeds the tree
of heaven.' "

When you kill an animal for food, reflect on the fact that you are both part of the natural world – part of a continual cycle of life and death. You, too, will give up your life one day, and your body will be food for the earth. In *The Prophet*'s poetic, hopeful understanding of the world, this sacrifice is fuel for the tree of heaven and a cycle of growth and return which is truly sacred.

"And when you crush an apple with
your teeth, say to it in
your heart,
'Your seeds shall live in my body,
And the buds of your tomorrow
shall blossom in my heart,
And your fragrance shall be my
breath, And together we shall
rejoice through all the seasons.'"

WHEN YOU EAT an apple, life is simply transferred from one living entity to another. It becomes part of you, it nourishes you. Its seeds live in your body, blossom in your heart and sweeten your breath.

The prophet Almustafa viewed eating animals no differently from eating fruits and vegetables – both are living things.

Time spent preparing, cooking and eating food is an opportunity to connect with and appreciate the food that you eat. When you prepare and eat your next meal today, think about where the food you are eating has come from. Imagine who may have grown or harvested it. How did it reach you?

“And in the autumn, when you
gather the grapes of your vineyards
for the winepress, say in your heart,
‘I too am a vineyard, and my fruit
shall be gathered for the winepress,
And like new wine I shall be kept
in eternal vessels.’
And in winter, when you draw the
wine, let there be in your heart a
song for each cup;
And let there be in the song a
remembrance for the autumn days,
and for the vineyard, and for
the winepress.”

SEE YOUR LIFE as being like tending a vineyard: your fruit – your experiences, your spirit, the essence of you – will grow and mature as it is harvested, stored, reflected upon and savored. Like wine it will be stored in vessels where it can be enjoyed as the seasons march on.

At the end of your life, reflect and be happy for all that you have lived, loved and experienced.

ON WORK

“Then a ploughman said, Speak to us of Work.

And he answered, saying:”

"You work that you may keep pace
with the earth and the soul of
the earth.
For to be idle is to become a
stranger unto the seasons, and to
step out of life's procession, that
marches in majesty and proud
submission towards the infinite.
When you work you are a
flute through whose heart the
whispering of the hours turns
to music.
Which of you would be a reed,
dumb and silent, when all else
sings together in unison?"

WORK IS A natural part of life that keeps us in rhythm and harmony with time and the seasons. To be idle is to be out of step with the world around you – "to step out of life's procession".

When you work, your efforts contribute to the good; they benefit everyone. Why would you want to be silent and unoccupied while everyone else works together in harmony?

“ Always you have been told that
work is a curse and labour
a misfortune.
But I say to you that when you
work you fulfil a part of earth’s
furthest dream, assigned to you
when that dream was born,
And in keeping yourself with
labour you are in truth loving life,
And to love life through labour is
to be intimate with life’s
inmost secret. ”

YOU MAY BELIEVE that work is a curse and a misfortune. But work is an opportunity to develop your potential and to contribute your unique skills, knowledge and abilities to the world.

Work provides meaning, purpose and fulfillment in your life. And when you have meaning and purpose, you will pour energy freely into the world – enriching the experience for everyone.

"And what is it to work with love?
It is to weave the cloth with
threads drawn from your heart,
even as if your beloved were to
wear that cloth.
It is to build a house with
affection, even as if your beloved
were to dwell in that house.
It is to sow seeds with tenderness
and reap the harvest with joy, even
as if your beloved were to eat
the fruit.
It is to charge all things you
fashion with a breath of your
own spirit."

To work with love is to do so unselfishly. Approach your work with a positive attitude; work as if you are doing it for someone you love and who will benefit directly from your labour. By doing so, your work is filled with your positive attitude and spirit.

> But what if you're stuck doing a job you really don't like? You find it boring and meaningless? Then do your best to find a way to make it more interesting. You have to decide for yourself that you're going to make your work meaningful. But if the job is just not you or it's too stressful, you should leave and find work that is more aligned with your abilities, interests and values.

“Often I have heard you say […]
‘He who works in marble, and
finds the shape of his own soul
in the stone, is nobler than he
who ploughs the soil. And he
who seizes the rainbow to lay it
on a cloth in the likeness of man,
is more than he who makes the
sandals for our feet.’
But I say […] that the wind speaks
not more sweetly to the giant oaks
than to the least of all the blades of
grass […].”

No one job, profession or role at work is more or less valuable, better or worse, worthy or unworthy than another. All hold the same value and importance: "the wind speaks not more sweetly to the giant oaks than to the least of all the blades of grass".

Whatever your job is, your work is contributing to the common good.

"Work is love made visible.
And if you cannot work with love
but only with distaste, it is better
that you should leave your work and
sit at the gate of the temple and take
alms of those who work with joy.
For if you bake bread with
indifference, you bake a bitter bread
that feeds but half man's hunger.
And if you grudge the crushing
of the grapes, your grudge distils
a poison in the wine. And if you
sing though as angels, and love
not the singing, you muffle man's
ears to the voices of the day and
the voices of the night."

"WORK IS LOVE made visible" – when you put all your heart and soul into your work it is charged with "the breath of your own spirit".

But if you can't work with love – with a positive attitude – it is better that you do nothing and receive what you need from those that are willing to work hard. For to work with dislike, with indifference or with a grudge taints – discredits and offends – both what you do and those you engage with.

The attitude you bring to your work affects you and everyone around you.

ON JOY AND SORROW

“ Then a woman said, Speak to us of Joy and Sorrow.

And he answered: ”

“ Your joy is your sorrow unmasked.
And the self-same well from which your laughter rises was oftentimes filled with your tears.
And how else can it be?
The deeper that sorrow carves into your being, the more joy you can contain.
Is not the cup that holds your wine the very cup that was burned in the potter's oven?
And is not the lute that soothes your spirit, the very wood that was hollowed with knives?
When you are joyous, look deep into your heart and you shall find it is only that which has given you sorrow that is giving you joy.
When you are sorrowful look again in your heart, and you shall see that in truth you are weeping for that which has been your delight. ”

"Your joy is your sorrow unmasked" – what gives you joy gives you sorrow; joy and sorrow come from the same source. The deeper your sorrow, the deeper your experience of joy.

In the process of being made, the cup for your wine and the lute that plays music have themselves experienced pain. The same is true for you: what gives you joy will also give you pain.

Whatever has been a source of joy and has made you happy has also been a source of sorrow and distress. And whatever has been a source of sadness has also been a source of joy.

> If you have loved, you will know this to be true: a partner, son or daughter, parent or friend is a source of joy but also a source of sorrow – frustration, worry, anguish, sadness and heartbreak.

"Some of you say, 'Joy is greater
than sorrow,' and others say, 'Nay,
sorrow is the greater.'
But I say unto you, they
are inseparable.
Together they come, and when one
sits alone with you at your board,
remember that the other is asleep
upon your bed.
Verily you are suspended like scales
between your sorrow and your joy.
Only when you are empty are you
at standstill and balanced."

Joy is no greater than sorrow, and sorrow is no greater than joy; they are intimately connected and do not exist in isolation – indeed they define and deepen each other. If sorrow is sitting with you and all seems lost, it is vital to know that joy is nearby – merely resting. Emotions are cyclical, not permanent.

You are always suspended on scales between sorrow and joy, and balanced only when empty.

ON HOUSES

“ Then a mason came forth and said,
Speak to us of Houses.
And he answered and said: ”

“Your house is your larger body. It grows in the sun and sleeps in the stillness of the night; and it is not dreamless.”

YOUR HOME IS an extension of yourself – of your body and mind. Just like you, it grows in the sun and sleeps in the night – it holds hope, desires and aspirations.

" What have you in these houses? And what
is it you guard with fastened doors?
Have you peace, the quiet urge that reveals
your power?
Have you remembrances, the glimmering arches
that span the summits of the mind?
Have you beauty, that leads the heart from
things fashioned of wood and stone to the
holy mountain?
Tell me, have you these in your houses?
Or have you only comfort, and the lust for
comfort, that stealthy thing that enters the
house a guest, and then becomes a host, and
then a master?
Verily the lust for comfort murders the passion of
the soul, and then walks grinning in the funeral.
[…]
You shall not dwell in tombs made by the dead
for the living. "

WHAT DO YOU have in your home; what is it that you guard with locked doors? Peace, memories, beauty and spirituality? A sense of being connected to something everlasting and larger than yourself? Is that what you have?

Or do you crave comfort – security, comfort and being in control? We all welcome comfort, but to remain in comfort leads to stagnation, and very soon you've lost your passion for and interest in life; you've become flat, dull and lifeless as if living in a tomb.

> Every time you make an excuse not to go out, your world shrinks. But if you can extend your comfort zone, you extend your beliefs about the world and what you're capable of.
>
> Think of three things you could do that would move you out of your comfort zone, things that won't involve too much of a stretch. Push yourself to do things a bit differently or to do more of them.
>
> For example, take a different route to work. Get off the bus or train one stop earlier and walk. Listen to a podcast or music you wouldn't normally listen to. Say yes to an invitation to do something you would usually say no to.

"But you, children of space, you restless in rest, you shall not be trapped nor tamed. Your house shall be not an anchor but a mast."

BUT "CHILDREN OF SPACE" – those of you who set out to explore and discover – your home doesn't hold you back and weigh you down like an anchor holds a ship. Instead, your home is like the ship's mast from which the sails unfold and open up to catch the wind and carry the ship on its way.

ON CLOTHES

"And the weaver said, Speak to us of Clothes.
And he answered: "

—

“ Your clothes conceal much of your
beauty, yet they hide not
the unbeautiful.
And though you seek in garments
the freedom of privacy you may
find in them a harness and a chain.
Would that you could meet the
sun and the wind with more of
your skin and less of your raiment. ”

Clothing conceals beauty but doesn't hide an unpleasant character. And although we may reach for clothes that provide privacy and protection, we may find them restrictive, like layers that separate us from our natural selves.

Let your body take pleasure more often from the feel of sun and wind on bare skin rather than the pleasure of being dressed up in fancy, formal clothes.

"Some of you say, 'It is the north
wind who has woven the clothes
we wear.'
And I say, Ay, it was the north wind,
But shame was his loom, and the
softening of the sinews was
his thread.
[...] Forget not that modesty is for a
shield against the eye of the unclean.
And when the unclean shall be no
more, what were modesty but a
fetter and a fouling of the mind?
And forget not that the earth
delights to feel your bare feet and the
winds long to play with your hair."

WE NEED CLOTHES for warmth and protection from the elements, but covering yourself up because you feel self-conscious makes you soft and weakens your spirit.

Modesty – covering up for the sake of decency – might hide your body from those with impure thoughts, yet when those people have gone, you still believe it's wrong – indecent even – not to cover yourself.

Remember: "the earth delights to feel your bare feet and the winds long to play with your hair".

ON BUYING AND SELLING

"And a merchant said, Speak to us of Buying and Selling.
And he answered and said: "

"To you the earth yields her fruit,
and you shall not want if you but
know how to fill your hands.
It is in exchanging the gifts of the
earth that you shall find abundance
and be satisfied.
Yet unless the exchange be in love
and kindly justice, it will but lead
some to greed and others
to hunger."

The earth provides everything you need; there is enough for everyone. No one will have too much, no one will go without. There will be no greed or hunger if you buy, sell and exchange the gifts of the earth with fairness, consideration and respect for each other.

“And suffer not the barren-handed
to take part in your transactions,
who would sell their words for
your labour.
To such men you should say,
‘Come with us to the field, or go
with our brothers to the sea and
cast your net;
For the land and the sea shall be
bountiful to you even as to us.’ ”

DON'T ALLOW ANYONE to come in empty – handed or to persuade you to give them something for nothing.

Tell them, instead, to join you in your place of work. Tell them that there they will find plenty for them, too.

“And if there come the singers and
the dancers and the flute players –
buy of their gifts also.
For they too are gatherers of fruit
and frankincense, and that which
they bring, though fashioned of
dreams, is raiment and food for
your soul.
And before you leave the
marketplace, see that no one has
gone his way with empty hands.”

THE SINGERS, DANCERS and musicians also have gifts to exchange. And though created from sounds and sensations, their contributions feed your spirit and soul. No one should leave the marketplace empty-handed.

ON CRIME AND PUNISHMENT

"Then one of the judges of the city stood forth and said, Speak to us of Crime and Punishment.
And he answered, saying: "

"Oftentimes have I heard you speak
of one who commits a wrong as
though he were not one of you,
but a stranger unto you and an
intruder upon your world.
But I say that even as the holy and
the righteous cannot rise beyond the
highest which is in each one of you,
So the wicked and the weak
cannot fall lower than the lowest
which is in you also.
And as a single leaf turns not
yellow but with the silent
knowledge of the whole tree, so
the wrongdoer cannot do wrong
without the hidden will of you all."

THE PERSON WHO commits a wrong is not a stranger – someone different from you – they are the same as you. The best of you is no better than the best in them. The worst of them is also the worst in you. A person can rise or fall no farther than those around them.

Just as a leaf can't turn yellow without the whole tree knowing about it, neither can a community be unaware of the wrongdoer's circumstances – the situation that led to their crime.

“Like a procession you walk
together towards your god-self.
You are the way and the wayfarers.
And when one of you falls down
he falls for those behind him, a
caution against the
stumbling stone.
Ay, and he falls for those ahead
of him, who though faster and
surer of foot, yet removed not the
stumbling stone.”

LIFE IS A shared journey, and we walk it together – each of us finding our way toward something deeper, truer, more whole.

When one person stumbles it serves as a warning and a lesson to those who follow. It also serves as a rebuke to those who are more steadfast but failed to look out for and remove anything that could make others stumble. Through collective effort we can make the way smoother – in this way, we are all connected: walkers, path-makers and learners.

" The righteous is not innocent of the
deeds of the wicked,
And the white-handed is not clean
in the doings of the felon.
Yea, the guilty is oftentimes the victim
of the injured,
And still more often the condemned is
the burden bearer for the guiltless
and unblamed.
You cannot separate the just from the unjust
and the good from the wicked;
For they stand together before the face of
the sun even as the black thread and the
white are woven together.
And when the black thread breaks, the
weaver shall look into the whole cloth,
and he shall examine the loom also. "

THOSE THAT ARE free from wrongdoing are not absolved; they aren't free from guilt or blame for crime.

The wrongdoer often takes all the blame, yet the victim and the criminal share responsibility for the crime; they are each part of the wrongdoing – and the problem – and are inextricably intertwined. When someone commits a crime, it's the structure of society that should be examined.

Crime can be seen to be the result of associated social problems – for example poverty, unemployment, discrimination and poor housing: "And when the black thread breaks, the weaver shall look into the whole cloth, and he shall examine the loom also."

" And you judges who would be just,
What judgment pronounce you
upon him who though honest in
the flesh yet is a thief in spirit?
What penalty lay you upon him
who slays in the flesh yet is himself
slain in the spirit?
And how prosecute you him who
in action is a deceiver and
an oppressor,
Yet who also is aggrieved
and outraged? "

THOSE OF YOU who would judge another, what judgment do you arrive at, what punishment do you mete out, when faced with someone who is essentially honest but whose good spirit has been crushed? How do you punish someone who has behaved dishonourably and yet is also a victim?

> Just as kindness is most likely to create more kindness, pain is most likely to produce more pain. Any action, whatever its nature, brings more of itself into the world.

"And how shall you punish those
whose remorse is already greater
than their misdeeds?
Is not remorse the justice which
is administered by that very law
which you would fain serve?
Yet you cannot lay remorse upon
the innocent nor lift it from the
heart of the guilty.
[…]
And you who would understand
justice, how shall you unless you
look upon all deeds in the fullness
of light?
[…]
Only then shall you know that the
erect and the fallen are but one
man standing in twilight."

HOW WOULD YOU punish someone who is now full of remorse and regret for their misdemeanour? Aren't their anguish and guilt punishment enough? The harshest punishment for crime is remorse when it falls on the heart of the guilty.

How can you mete out justice unless you take into consideration all the circumstances that led to the crime? Justice requires understanding and compassion; you will know this when you accept that each of us – the virtuous and the wrongdoer – is "standing in twilight", a space in which moral strength is often waning.

The prophet's advice also applies to our approach towards someone who has offended, hurt or upset us in some way.

Rather than seek revenge and punishment, it may be better to forgive. Forgiveness is for you and not the other person. It means letting go of the resentment and anger and no longer wanting punishment, revenge or compensation.

Forgiving doesn't mean excusing or forgetting the offence. The other person is still responsible for their actions, but you deserve to be free of this pain and resentment.

Start by acknowledging how you feel – are you angry, upset, disappointed?

Try to understand why they did what they did. But know that you may not ever know; you don't have to know why something happened in order to let go.

Write the wrongdoer a letter that you may or may not send. Say everything you couldn't say to them: how their actions made you feel, how you were affected and what, if anything, they can do to make amends.

Think back to anyone who might have helped and supported you when you suffered the wrongdoing. Thinking in this way – directing your mind to the positive aspects of the event – can help interrupt angry, bitter thoughts.

ON LAW

" Then a lawyer said, But what of our Laws, master?
And he answered: "

—

" You delight in laying down laws,
Yet you delight more in
breaking them.
Like children playing by the ocean who build
sand-towers with constancy and then destroy
them with laughter.
[…] But what of those […] to whom life is
a rock, and the law a chisel with which they
would carve it in their own likeness? What of
the cripple who hates dancers?
What of the ox who loves his yoke and deems the
elk and deer of the forest stray and vagrant things?
What of the old serpent who cannot shed his
skin, and calls all others naked and shameless?
[…] What shall I say of these save that they too
stand in the sunlight, but with their backs to
the sun?
They see only their shadows, and their shadows
are their laws. "

Some people make and break laws and rules on a whim – whenever it suits them. And then there are those people who only make laws and rules to suit their own purposes and condemn those who don't abide by them. Although those who make the rules and laws "stand in the sunlight" – live with freedom and happiness – they turn their backs to it and cast a shadow that others must live in.

When lawmakers are mean and petty, selfish and controlling, indifferent or opposed to what brings happiness to others, their laws and rules reflect this. And instead of guiding others, those laws become chains.

"But you who walk facing the sun, what images drawn on the earth can hold you? You who travel with the wind, what weathervane shall direct your course? What man's law shall bind you if you break your yoke but upon no man's prison door? What laws shall you fear if you dance but stumble against no man's iron chains? And who is he that shall bring you to judgment if you tear off your garment yet leave it in no man's path? People of Orphalese, you can muffle the drum, and you can loosen the strings of the lyre, but who shall command the skylark not to sing?"

BUT THOSE OF you who are free-spirited and happy, can laws and rules tell you what you can and cannot do? What man-made rules and laws can constrain you if your actions do no harm to others?

As much as anyone might try to subdue you, no law can hold you. Like the skylark, you are free to soar into the sky and sing.

> The prophet is not suggesting that people should break the law and ignore the rules; rather he is pointing out that there is a difference between man-made and natural laws. The laws of nature are the moral principles – the sense of right and wrong that guides a person's thoughts and actions – that, in an ideal world, would be the only laws necessary.

ON FREEDOM

“And an orator said, Speak
to us of Freedom.
And he answered: ”

—

" [...] I have seen the freest among
you wear their freedom as a yoke
and a handcuff.
And my heart bled within me; for
you can only be free when [...] you
cease to speak of freedom as a goal
and a fulfilment.
You shall be free indeed when your
days are not without a care nor
your nights without a want
and a grief,
But rather when these things
girdle your life and yet you rise
above them naked and unbound. "

YOUR PURSUIT OF freedom oppresses and restrains you. You can only be free when you stop craving freedom – when you cease to see freedom as something to achieve.

You think you will be free when your days and nights are free of worry and anxiety, without want or fear and sorrow. It's your pursuit of freedom from worry and fear that confines you. You'll only be free when you've learned to accept and live *with* worries, wants, fears and sorrows – they are unavoidable – and rise above them.

“And how shall you rise beyond your days and nights unless you break the chains which you at the dawn of your understanding have fastened around your noon hour? In truth that which you call freedom is the strongest of these chains, though its links glitter in the sun and dazzle your eyes. And what is it but fragments of your own self you would discard that you may become free?”

How shall you be free of your fears and worries when it's your beliefs about freedom that are chaining you?

As attractive as freedom is, the conditions you wish to escape – worry, want and grief – are part of the human experience. You cannot rid yourself of them.

“And if it is a care you would cast off, that care has been chosen by you rather than imposed upon you. And if it is a fear you would dispel, the seat of that fear is in your heart and not in the hand of the feared.”

If you wish to free yourself from worry and fear, remember: you do have a choice. No one can *make* you feel anxious. It is how you respond that gives fear its power.

And if you long to be free of fear, understand that it doesn't arise from the object you fear, but from how you hold it in your heart and mind.

If something feels like a heavy burden, gently ask yourself whether you might have taken it on by choice – without even realizing it. You may find that you've accepted or internalized it, and in recognizing this, you might begin to release it.

“Verily all things move within your being in constant half embrace, the desired and the dreaded, the repugnant and the cherished, the pursued and that which you would escape.
These things move within you as lights and shadows in pairs that cling.
And when the shadow fades and is no more, the light that lingers becomes a shadow to another light.”

All that you want and don't want come together "in constant half embrace" like light and shadow.

And when you transcend – rise above – fear or worry, you move towards a greater understanding, where freedom is to be found. True freedom is a transcendent state of being. Although the concerns, worries and fears are still present, the truly free person has risen above them.

ON REASON AND PASSION

"And the priestess spoke again and said: Speak to us of Reason and Passion.

And he answered, saying: "

"Your soul is oftentimes a battlefield, upon which your reason and your judgment wage war against your passion and your appetite.
[...] Your reason and your passion are the rudder and the sails of your seafaring soul.
If either your sails or your rudder be broken, you can but toss and drift, or else be held at a standstill in mid-seas. For reason, ruling alone, is a force confining; and passion, unattended, is a flame that burns to its own destruction."

REASON AND EMOTION – your head and your heart – are often opposing each other. Your head – reason – tries to outdo your heart, and your heart – your emotions – tries to overwhelm your head.

But reason and emotions are like the rudder and sails of a ship: the rudder – reasoning and rationalizing – guides you while the sails – feelings and emotions – inspire and move you. Without reason you would be drifting uncontrollably. Without emotion you would be at a standstill. On its own, reason can limit and restrict you. And left to their own devices, strong feelings and emotions can overwhelm you and become destructive.

> The prophet Almustafa is explaining what we now know as emotional intelligence. Emotional intelligence involves using your emotions and feelings to inform your thoughts and using your thoughts to inform your emotions and feelings. In other words, it's using your head to guide your heart and your heart to guide your head.

"Therefore let your soul exalt your
reason to the height of passion,
that it may sing;
And let it direct your passion with
reason, that your passion may live
through its own daily resurrection,
and like the phoenix rise above
its own ashes.
[...] You too should rest in reason
and move in passion."

LET YOUR EMOTIONS lift your reasoning – your thoughts and beliefs – to great heights. And let reason dignify and guide your emotions so that they may rise above themselves and emerge reborn.

Be calm and at peace when reasoning and be inspired by your emotions: "rest in reason and move in passion".

ON PAIN

“ And a woman spoke, saying,
Tell us of Pain.
And he said: ”

“Your pain is the breaking of
the shell that encloses your
understanding.
Even as the stone of the fruit must
break, that its heart may stand in
the sun, so must you know pain.
And could you keep your heart
in wonder at the daily miracles of
your life, your pain would not seem
less wondrous than your joy;
And you would accept the seasons
of your heart, even as you have
always accepted the seasons that
pass over your fields.
And you would watch with
serenity through the winters of
your grief.”

WITH PAIN – EMOTIONAL pain – comes a realization, an understanding of a truth. You learn something new. Just as the stone of a fruit must be released and exposed to the sun if it is to grow, so personal growth can follow pain.

As you marvel at the wonder of joy, so marvel at the wonder of pain and sorrow. And just as you accept the vagaries and the passing of the seasons on the fields, accept the vagaries of your heart. The heart has its seasons, and pain and sorrow are its winter. Accept this with grace.

The prophet suggests that whenever you experience emotional pain, you can learn from it.

Although emotions such as guilt, regret and disappointment might be painful, they do have a positive purpose: they prompt you to reflect on what you have learned from a specific experience and what you might do differently in a similar situation in the future.

ON SELF-KNOWLEDGE

"And a man said, Speak to us of Self-Knowledge.
And he answered, saying:"

" Your hearts know in silence the
secrets of the days and the nights.
But your ears thirst for the sound
of your heart's knowledge.
You would know in words that
which you have always known
in thought.
You would touch with your fingers
the naked body of your dream
And it is well you should.
The hidden wellspring of your
soul must needs rise and run
murmuring to the sea;
And the treasure of your infinite
depths would be revealed to
your eyes. "

In your heart, your thoughts and dreams reside in silence. But your spirit wants to express what it knows and to be heard. Your "hidden wellspring" of knowledge must be tapped and the infinite depths of your knowledge revealed to you.

What "your heart knows in silence" may be an aspect of self-awareness we know as intuition: a direct perception of a truth. Intuition bridges the gap between the conscious reasoning and the non-conscious parts of your mind.

Intuition is the unexpressed silence, thoughts and dreams that the prophet speaks of that rise into your consciousness with sound, words and touch. So often, your intuition is drowned out by all the other noise and activity going on in your head. In future, when you feel your intuition is speaking to you, ignore external distractions and interruptions so that you can tune into the true feelings, thoughts, words and images that come into your mind.

"Say not, 'I have found the truth',
but rather, 'I have found a truth.'
Say not, 'I have found the path of
the soul.' Say rather, 'I have met
the soul walking upon my path.'
For the soul walks upon all paths.
The soul walks not upon a line,
neither does it grow like a reed.
The soul unfolds itself, like a lotus
of countless petals."

Don't think that there's one single truth about yourself and the world around you. There is no one right answer, no definitive way to be.

What you learn is not the same for everyone; there's always more than one meaning, more than one way of understanding, more than one path and more than one direction. There are countless possibilities "like a lotus of countless petals" that unfold and open up to you.

ON TEACHING

“Then said a teacher, Speak
to us of Teaching.
And he said: ”

—

“No man can reveal to you aught
but that which already lies half
asleep in the dawning of
your knowledge.
The teacher who walks in the
shadow of the temple, among his
followers, gives not of his wisdom
but rather of his faith and
his lovingness.
If he is indeed wise he does not
bid you enter the house of his
wisdom, but rather leads you to the
threshold of your own mind.”

No one can teach you anything except that which already exists just below your level of conscious awareness. A good teacher doesn't tell you what they know; rather they lead you to a place where learning can begin and you can find out for yourself. A teacher facilitates learning, supports you and believes in your ability to discover, learn and understand things for yourself.

"The astronomer may speak to you of his understanding of space, but he cannot give you his understanding.
The musician may sing to you of the rhythm which is in all space, but he cannot give you the ear which arrests the rhythm nor the voice that echoes it. And he who is versed in the science of numbers can tell of the regions of weight and measure, but he cannot conduct you thither.
For the vision of one man lends not its wings to another man."

ANOTHER PERSON CAN tell you what they understand and know, but they cannot pass on their wisdom and understanding.

The prophet Almustafa is talking about the difference between knowledge and wisdom. Knowledge involves knowing truths and facts, rules and principles. Wisdom is concerned with knowing how and when to use what you know. It's making meaning of the truths and facts, rules and principles that you know.

Wisdom is a result of learning from and reflecting on your personal experience. Another person cannot, therefore, pass on their wisdom because "the vision of one man lends not its wings [its wisdom] to another man".

ON FRIENDSHIP

" And a youth said, Speak
to us of Friendship.
And he answered, saying: "

—

"Your friend is your
needs answered.
He is your field which you sow
with love and reap
with thanksgiving.
And he is your board and
your fireside.
For you come to him with your
hunger, and you seek him
for peace."

IN FRIENDSHIP, "YOU sow with love and reap with thanksgiving": you get out of a friendship what you put in. A true friend meets your deeper needs – not just for company or shared interests, but for comfort, nourishment and peace.

"When your friend speaks his
mind you fear not the 'nay' in
your own mind, nor do you
withhold the 'ay'.
And when he is silent your heart
ceases not to listen to his heart;
For without words, in friendship,
all thoughts, all desires, all
expectations are born and shared,
with joy that is unacclaimed.
When you part from your friend,
you grieve not;
For that which you love most in
him may be clearer in his absence,
as the mountain to the climber is
clearer from the plain."

FRIENDS CAN SPEAK to each other without fear; they feel free to disagree or agree. Words aren't always necessary; friendship rises above spoken words. When a friend is silent, you are still there for them. You simply know their heart's thoughts, desires and expectations with your own heart, with no need for words or announcements.

When you are apart, you're not sad; rather, in your friend's absence you see more clearly that which you love in them – "as the mountain to the climber is clearer from the plain".

“And let your best be for
your friend.
If he must know the ebb of your
tide, let him know its flood also.
For what is your friend that you
should seek him with hours to kill?
Seek him always with hours to live.
[…] And in the sweetness of
friendship let there be laughter,
and sharing of pleasures.
For in the dew of little things the
heart finds its morning and
is refreshed.”

Be your best for your friend. As well as turning to them in your misfortune, share the good times, too – the highs and lows of your life.

Don't just spend time with them when it's convenient and you have time to spare – "hours to kill" – prioritize your time with them – the "hours to live" – and make that time special and important. Laugh and have fun together. It's the small pleasures that you share that will renew your spirit and invigorate you.

ON TALKING

"And then a scholar said,
Speak of Talking.
And he answered, saying:"

—

“ And there are those who talk, and
without knowledge or forethought
reveal a truth which they
themselves do not understand.
And there are those who have the
truth within them, but they tell it
not in words.
In the bosom of such as these the
spirit dwells in rhythmic silence. ”

Some people speak without thinking and unintentionally touch on something true, while others who do not feel the need to hold forth are quietly confident in their knowledge and perception. These unstarry people are in tune with something greater, and their silence is not ignorance – it's depth.

“When you meet your friend on
the roadside or in the marketplace,
let the spirit in you move your lips
and direct your tongue.
Let the voice within your voice
speak to the ear of his ear;
For his soul will keep the truth of
your heart as the taste of the wine
is remembered
When the colour is forgotten and
the vessel is no more.”

WHEN YOU'RE TALKING with a friend, let your heart and spirit – "the voice within your voice" – guide what your friend hears you say. Be sincere and genuine because what they hear you say will be long remembered.

ON TIME

" And an astronomer said, Master, what of Time?
And he answered: "

—

"You would measure time the measureless and the immeasurable. You would adjust your conduct and even direct the course of your spirit according to hours and seasons. Of time you would make a stream upon whose bank you would sit and watch its flowing. Yet the timeless in you is aware of life's timelessness, And knows that yesterday is but today's memory and tomorrow is today's dream."

ALTHOUGH YOU CAN'T measure time, you act as a time-keeper. In measuring, dividing and living your life around the days, months and years, you attempt to direct the course of time as you would the flow of a river.

And yet the timeless in you – your spirit – knows that time is continuous and boundless; that yesterday is "today's memory and tomorrow is today's dream".

The present doesn't stand alone: it's informed by experience from the past, as the future is by experience from the present, its own past.

“And that that which sings and contemplates in you is still dwelling within the bounds of that first moment which scattered the stars into space. Who among you does not feel that his power to love is boundless?

And yet who does not feel that very love, though boundless, encompassed within the centre of his being, and moving not from love thought to love thought, nor from love deeds to other love deeds?

And is not time even as love is, undivided and paceless?

But if in your thought you must measure time into seasons, let each season encircle all the other seasons,

And let today embrace the past with remembrance and the future with longing.”

And yet your spirit is as it was at the beginning of time. Just as time is boundless, so the love in your heart – in the centre of your being – is boundless. It is not measured by the number of loving thoughts and acts you experience, it is "undivided and paceless".

But if you must measure time, let the past, present and future come together as one. And look back on the past with good memories and look to the future with hope.

ON GOOD AND EVIL

" And one of the elders of the city said, Speak to us of Good and Evil.

And he answered: "

" Of the good in you I can speak,
but not of the evil.
For what is evil but good tortured
by its own hunger and thirst?
Verily when good is hungry it
seeks food even in dark caves, and
when it thirsts it drinks even of
dead waters. "

HERE EVIL IS not the opposite of good but rather what happens when good loses its way under pressure. When our goodness is starved, it might find its way into dark, dangerous places – and do desperate things to survive.

"You are good when you are one
with yourself.
Yet when you are not one with
yourself you are not evil.
For a divided house is not a den of
thieves; it is only a divided house.
And a ship without rudder may
wander aimlessly among perilous
isles yet sink not to the bottom."

You are good when you are at one with yourself – in tune with your mind, body and spirit – and have no conflicting needs or wants pulling you in an opposing direction. When you're not at one with yourself, you're not evil but divided; you are compromised and without direction.

“ You are good when you strive to give
of yourself.
Yet you are not evil when you seek gain
for yourself.
[...]
You are good when you are fully awake in
your speech,
Yet you are not evil when you sleep while
your tongue staggers
without purpose.
[...]
You are good when you walk to your goal
firmly and with
bold steps.
Yet you are not evil when you go
thither limping [...].
You are good in countless ways, and you
are not evil when you are not good. ”

You are good when you give of yourself but not evil if you seek to gain for yourself. You are good when you are thoughtful and conscious of what you say, but you are not evil if you hesitate to speak or are unclear about what you are saying.

You are good when you are purposeful, bold and courageous. But you are not evil if you are reluctant to act and you hold back. You are good in many ways, and you are not evil when you are not good.

When it comes to understanding the nature of evil, the prophet's key message is that evil is not the opposite of good. He suggests that "evil" occurs as a result of mitigating circumstances, of events – "hunger and thirst" – that are often outside a person's control and which lead them to commit wrongdoings.

ON PRAYER

" Then a priestess said, Speak to us of Prayer.

And he answered, saying: "

“You pray in your distress and in your need; would that you might pray also in the fullness of your joy and in your days of abundance.

For what is prayer but the expansion of yourself into the living ether?

And if it is for your comfort to pour your darkness into space, it is also for your delight to pour forth the dawning of your heart.

And if you cannot but weep when your soul summons you to prayer, she should spur you again and yet again, though weeping, until you shall come laughing.”

YOU PRAY IN times of distress and need but you should also pray in times of joy and abundance. For what is prayer but "the expansion of yourself into the living ether": your awareness expanding and communing with the heavens.

If, in the darkness, you reach out to the heavens for comfort and reassurance, you should also pray – pour out your light – when you are content and happy.

And if you can't help but pray in sorrow and distress, use prayer to wring out your tears, to keep praying until you feel better again.

Whether or not you are someone who prays, by consciously acknowledging and showing gratitude for the good things, events and people in your life, you also encourage your own happiness and well-being.

At the end of each day, identify three good things that have happened that day. You might want to write them down in a journal or simply reflect on what those things are just before you go to sleep.

Appreciate knowing that you had good in your day, so that whatever the difficulties you are facing, you did in fact have things that made it all worthwhile. Instead of dwelling on what wasn't right, get into the habit of noticing and reflecting on the small pleasures – what was good and right about your day – instead. It could simply be that you had something good to eat, that the sun shone, or that you received a supportive message from someone.

By the end of the week you will know that 21 positive things happened.

"When you pray you rise to meet in the air those who are praying at that very hour, and whom save in prayer you may not meet.
Therefore let your visit to that temple invisible be for naught but ecstasy and sweet communion.
For if you should enter the temple for no other purpose than asking you shall not receive:
And if you should enter into it to humble yourself you shall not be lifted:
Or even if you should enter into it to beg for the good of others you shall not be heard.
It is enough that you enter the temple invisible."

When you pray, you rise to meet in spirit those who are also praying at that time. There's no need to make yourself known, or to ask for what you want; it's enough just that you are there, unknown to others, experiencing a wordless communion – a sharing of thoughts or feelings – in the presence of others. Truly, a shared spiritual experience.

ON PLEASURE

" Then a hermit, who visited the city
once a year, came forth and said,
Speak to us of Pleasure.
And he answered, saying: "

"Pleasure is a freedom-song,
But it is not freedom.
It is the blossoming of your desires,
But it is not their fruit.
It is a depth calling unto a height,
But it is not the deep nor the high.
It is the caged taking wing,
But it is not space encompassed.
Ay, in very truth, pleasure
is a freedom-song.
And I fain would have you sing it
with fullness of heart; yet I would
not have you lose your hearts
in the singing."

PLEASURE IS A song of freedom. It's not freedom from fears and worries, it's the realization of your dreams, something deep within you that reaches out and flies. Sing the freedom-song with "fullness of heart" – with enthusiasm – but without getting so carried away that you lose your heart.

We all have things that we enjoy, that give us pleasure. It might be time with family or a shared interest with friends, a holiday or a music event. Small things can give you pleasure, too. Maybe, for you, it's eating a perfectly ripe peach or pear. Perhaps a bubble bath or a hot shower and a warm towel to dry yourself? Or reading a book by one of your favourite authors or playing loud music and singing along to it while you cook dinner? Or sharing a pizza with someone you love? Sitting in the sun or a walk in the rain? Maybe talking to your dog or cat is one of your small pleasures?

Make a list of small pleasures and favourite things and do them more often. Add to your list every time you think of something else that brings a small pleasure.

"Some of your youth seek pleasure as if it
were all, and they are judged and rebuked.
I would not judge nor rebuke them.
I would have them seek.
[...]
And some of your elders remember pleasures
with regret like wrongs committed
in drunkenness.
But regret is the beclouding of the mind and
not its chastisement.
They should remember their pleasures with
gratitude, as they would the harvest
of a summer.
[...]
And there are among you those who are neither
young to seek nor old to remember;
And in their fear of seeking and remembering
they shun all pleasures, lest they neglect the
spirit or offend against it.
But even in their foregoing is their pleasure."

Some young people might get carried away in their pursuit of pleasure. Leave them to do so; there's no need to judge them or rebuke them for it.

Some older people look back on their pleasures with regret, but regret isn't helpful. Better to reminisce with gratitude and be thankful for the pleasures you've experienced.

And then there are some people who avoid seeking or remembering pleasure for fear it will harm their spirit. But the abstaining from pleasure is in itself a pleasure.

" Oftentimes in denying yourself
pleasure you do but store the desire
in the recesses of your being.
Who knows but that which seems
omitted today, waits for tomorrow?
Even your body knows its heritage
and its rightful need and will not
be deceived.
And your body is the harp
of your soul,
And it is yours to bring forth sweet
music from it or confused sounds. "

WHEN YOU DENY yourself pleasure, the desire for pleasure is still there, but the opportunity for today's pleasure may be gone by tomorrow.

Even though you've suppressed it, your body is not deceived; it knows that your need for pleasure is inherent. Your body is an instrument of pleasure, so allow it to enjoy pleasure.

“ And now you ask in your heart,
‘How shall we distinguish that which
is good in pleasure from that which
is not good?’
Go to your fields and your gardens, and
you shall learn that it is the pleasure of
the bee to gather honey of the flower,
But it is also the pleasure of the flower
to yield its honey to the bee.
For to the bee a flower is a
fountain of life,
And to the flower a bee is a
messenger of love,
And to both, bee and flower, the giving
and the receiving of pleasure is a need
and an ecstasy.
People of Orphalese, be in your pleasures
like the flowers and the bees. ”

IF YOU'RE WONDERING what is and isn't good pleasure, know that just as the bee enjoys the nectar it gathers from the flower and the flower enjoys giving nectar to the bee, you can be the same: happy to please other people and happy to receive pleasures that other people give. For "the giving and the receiving of pleasure is a need and an ecstasy".

ON BEAUTY

" And a poet said, Speak
to us of Beauty.
And he answered: "

“Where shall you seek beauty, and
how shall you find her unless she
herself be your way and
your guide?
And how shall you speak of her
except she be the weaver
of your speech?”

Once you've experienced beauty, you'll recognize beauty whenever you come across it – and you will witness and speak of it with reverence. But you will not be able to hunt it down or capture it, for true beauty appears not to those who search for it, but to those who are guided by it.

"The aggrieved and the injured say, 'Beauty is
kind and gentle.
Like a young mother half-shy of her own glory
she walks among us.'
And the passionate say, 'Nay, beauty is a thing
of might and dread.
Like the tempest she shakes the earth beneath us
and the sky above us.'
The tired and the weary say, 'Beauty is of soft whisperings.
She speaks in our spirit. Her voice yields to our silences
like a faint light that quivers in fear of the shadow.'
But the restless say, 'We have heard her shouting
among the mountains,
And with her cries came the sound of hoofs, and the
beating of wings and the roaring of lions.'
[...]
In winter say the snow-bound, 'She shall come with
the spring leaping upon the hills.'
And in the summer heat the reapers say, 'We have seen
her dancing with the autumn leaves, and we saw a drift of
snow in her hair.' All these things have you said of beauty,
Yet in truth you spoke not of her but of needs unsatisfied,
And beauty is not a need but an ecstasy.
It is not a mouth thirsting nor an empty hand
stretched forth,
a heart enflamed and a soul enchanted."

BEAUTY IS SOMETHING different for everyone and can be described in different ways: "kind and gentle" or "a thing of might and dread"; "soft whisperings" or the "shouting among the mountains". It might be the rising or the setting of the sun and the arrival of spring or autumn and winter. Although these events may be described as being things of beauty, they are not. They are unmet needs. Beauty is not a need, it is simply a joy and a delight.

"Beauty is eternity gazing at itself
in a mirror.
But you are eternity and you
are the mirror."

THE BEAUTY YOU see and experience in the outside world is simply a reflection of your own inner beauty. The mirror reflects the beauty in the outside world as your inner beauty sees it.

> Beauty can be found in shapes and colours, designs and patterns. It can be found in a view – a landscape, a cityscape or a seascape. Beauty can be found in art and architecture, a poem, a painting, a person, a face. Beauty can be found in a sound – music and song, the wind and rain.
>
> An awareness and appreciation of beauty can give you a sense of calm and peace. Beauty is uplifting and inspiring. What do you perceive to be beautiful? What sights and sounds, tastes and smells please you? Consciously look for and appreciate instances of the beauty of which we are naturally a part: music, literature and art, wildlife or other miracles of nature.

ON RELIGION

"And an old priest said, Speak to us of Religion.

And he said:"

“ Is not religion all deeds and
all reflection,
And that which is neither deed
nor reflection, but a wonder and a
surprise ever springing in the soul. ”

Religion lives in all you do and think – but it is also more than that. It is the wonder that rises unbidden in the soul that reminds you there is something deeper than reason and action.

"He who wears his morality but
as his best garment were
better naked.
[...]
And he who defines his conduct
by ethics imprisons his songbird
in a cage.
The freest song comes not through
bars and wires.
And he to whom worshipping is a
window, to open but also to shut,
has not yet visited the house of
his soul whose windows are from
dawn to dawn."

It's not necessary to make a point of showing other people that you're a good person by conforming to the "right" rules of conduct. Ethical conduct has no rules.

The expression of your spirit is not something to be restrained, and the act of worship is not something that is open and closed. Your church is within you, and so your access to worship is always available, "from dawn to dawn".

“ And if you would know God be not therefore a solver of riddles. Rather look about you and you shall see Him playing with your children.

And look into space; you shall see Him walking in the cloud, outstretching His arms in the lightning and descending in rain. You shall see Him smiling in flowers, then rising and waving His hands in trees. ”

GOD IS NOT complicated or hidden; He is not difficult to understand. To know God is to simply recognize and experience Him in the world; playing with children, in the skies, in the lightning and rain, and throughout nature, in the flowers and the trees.

ON DEATH

" Then Almitra spoke, saying,
We would ask now of Death.
And he said: "

—

"You would know the secret
of death.
But how shall you find it unless
you seek it in the heart of life?
[...]
If you would indeed behold the
spirit of death, open your heart
wide unto the body of life.
For life and death are one, even as
the river and the sea are one."

THE MYSTERY OF death is to be found in the heart of life. But how will you know that unless you embrace life and live it to the full? Just as we can't separate the river from the sea, we can't separate life from death. Death is part of life.

" For what is it to die but to stand
naked in the wind and to melt into
the sun?
And what is it to cease breathing
but to free the breath from its
restless tides, that it may rise
and expand and seek God
unencumbered?
Only when you drink from the river
of silence shall you indeed sing.
And when you have reached the
mountain top, then you shall begin
to climb.
And when the earth shall claim
your limbs, then shall you
truly dance. "

To DIE IS to be released from all earthly concerns. Although death is an end to life, death is the beginning of something new. "Only when you drink from the river of silence shall you indeed sing" – only when you cease to fear death will you enjoy living; the secret of death is to let go of fear, so that we may enjoy life.

And when you die – "when you drink from the river of silence [...] when you have reached the mountain top [...] when the earth shall claim your limbs" – you shall rise up into eternity and your spirit will be free to rejoice.

THE FAREWELL

“And now it was evening.
And Almitra the seeress said,
Blessed be this day and this place
and your spirit that has spoken.
And he answered, Was it I who
spoke? Was I not also a listener?
Then he descended the steps of the
Temple and all the people followed
him. And he reached his ship and
stood upon the deck.
And facing the people again, he
raised his voice and said:
People of Orphalese, the wind bids
me leave you.
Less hasty am I than the wind, yet
I must go.”

" You have been told that, even like a chain, you are as weak as your weakest link.
This is but half the truth.
You are also as strong as your strongest link.
To measure you by your smallest deed is to reckon the power of ocean by the frailty of its foam.
To judge you by your failures is to cast blame upon the seasons for their inconstancy.
[...]
I only speak to you in words of that which you yourselves know in thought.
And what is word knowledge but a shadow of wordless knowledge? "

YOU MAY BE as weak as the weakest part of yourselves, but you are as strong as the strongest part. Being judged by your smallest deeds is like judging the power of the ocean by the foam it produces. To criticize your failures is like blaming the seasons for their variability.

These are things you already know; at some point this "wordless knowledge" will become clear to you.

Also available as part of the Timeless Wisdom series

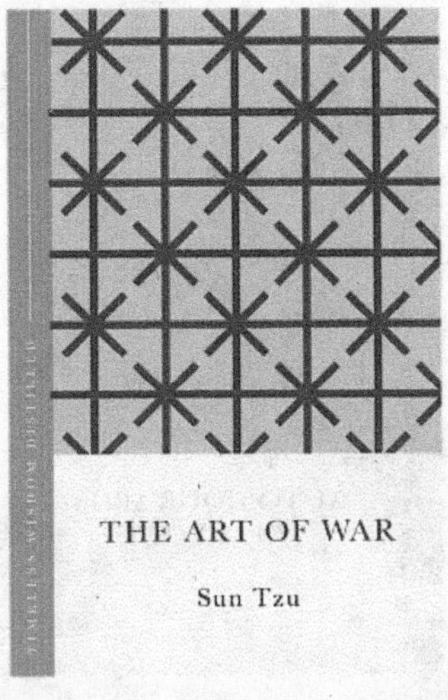

The Art of War: Timeless Wisdom Distilled **by Sun Tzu**

Master strategy, sharpen your thinking, and lead with purpose.

The Art of War is the ultimate guide to strategy, foresight and adaptability. Written over 2,000 years ago, Sun Tzu's wisdom has been used by leaders across disciplines to outthink their rivals, navigate conflict and act with precision and purpose.

This distilled edition draws out the most essential lessons from the text and pairs them with sharp, relevant commentary by bestselling author Gill Hasson. Whether you're facing personal or professional challenges, this is your concise manual for achieving clarity and success.

Hardback ISBN: 978 1 399 82150 6
Ebook ISBN: 978 1 399 82151 3

For more information, please visit www.johnmurraypress.co.uk

Also available as part of the Timeless Wisdom series

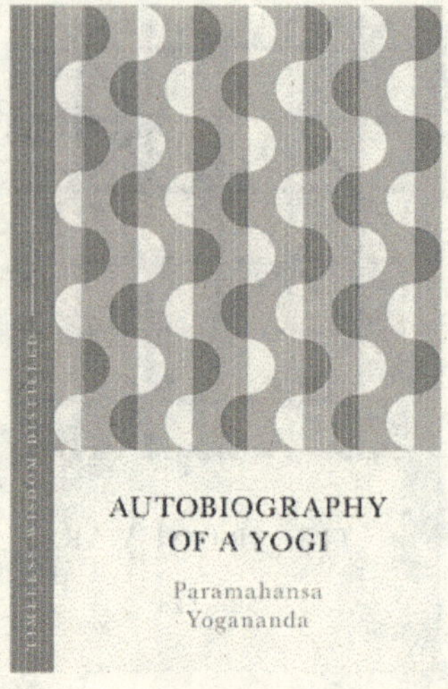

Autobiography of a Yogi: Timeless Wisdom Distilled
by Paramahansa Yogananda

Embark on a journey of spiritual discovery and inner transformation.

In his extraordinary *Autobiography of a Yogi*, Paramahansa Yogananda shares a visionary account of his life, teachings and encounters with saints, sages and seekers. A gateway into India's spiritual heritage, it is one of the most influential memoirs of the 20th century.

This distilled edition features the most powerful teachings from the original text, accompanied by illuminating commentary from best-selling author Gill Hasson. Deeply inspiring and accessible, it invites you to explore a life of purpose, connection and selfrealization.

Hardback ISBN: 978 1 399 82152 0
Ebook ISBN: 978 1 399 82153 7

For more information, please visit www.johnmurraypress.co.uk

Also available as part of the Timeless Wisdom series

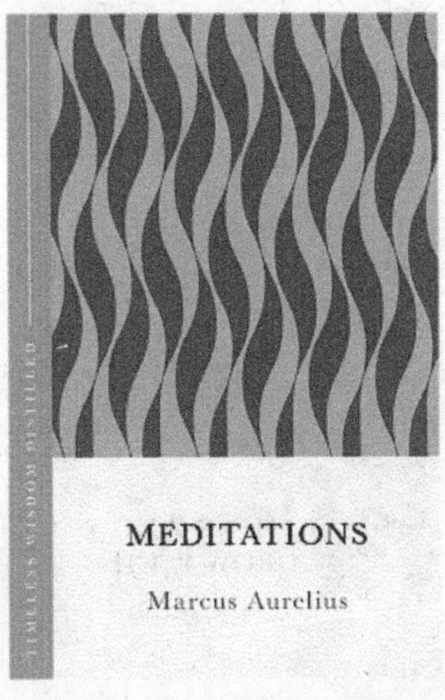

Meditations: Timeless Wisdom Distilled **by Marcus Aurelius**

Find clarity, resilience and purpose in turbulent times.

Roman emperor and Stoic philosopher Marcus Aurelius's *Meditations* is a profound and personal guide to living with integrity, courage and calm. His reflections remain strikingly relevant, speaking across the centuries to anyone seeking a more meaningful and grounded life.

This distilled edition presents his most powerful insights, accompanied by fresh, accessible commentary from bestselling author Gill Hasson. A wise and practical companion for everyday life, this book will help you build inner strength and live in accordance with your highest values.

Hardback ISBN: 978 1 399 82148 3
Ebook ISBN: 978 1 399 82149 0

For more information, please visit www.johnmurraypress.co.uk

Also available as part of the Timeless Wisdom series

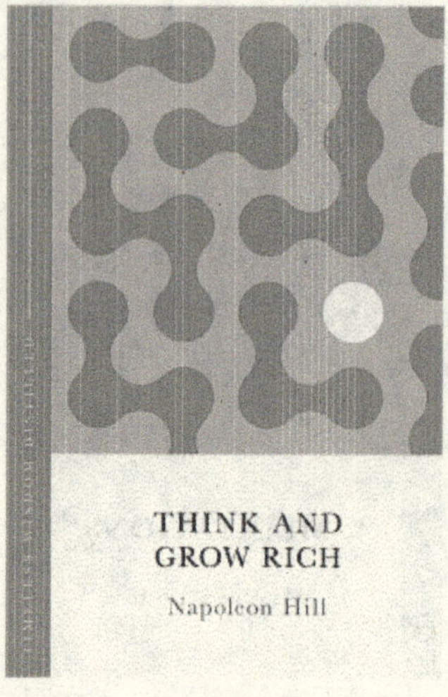

Think and Grow Rich: Timeless Wisdom Distilled by Napoleon Hill

Discover the power of your thoughts to shape your destiny.

Think and Grow Rich is Napoleon Hill's timeless guide to achieving personal and financial success. Drawing on the insights of history's most successful figures, it sets out a practical blueprint for turning desire into achievement through belief, persistence and focused thought.

This distilled edition features all of the original's most powerful lessons, paired with fresh and revealing commentary from bestselling author Gill Hasson. Clear, compelling and deeply relevant today, it's your essential guide to unlocking your potential and creating the life you want.

Hardback ISBN: 978 1 473 63626 2
Ebook ISBN: 978 1 473 63627 9

For more information, please visit www.johnmurraypress.co.uk

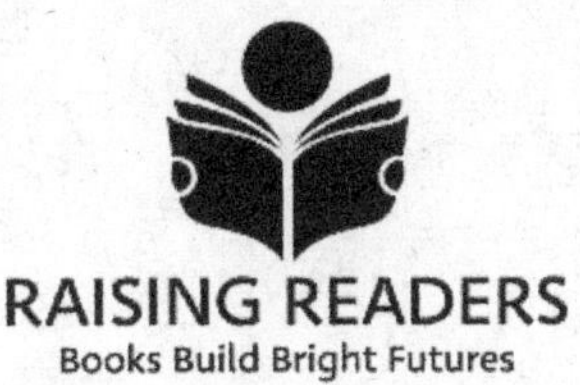

RAISING READERS
Books Build Bright Futures

Dear Reader,

We'd love your attention for one more page to tell you about the crisis in children's reading, and what we can all do.

Studies have shown that reading for fun is the **single biggest predictor of a child's future life chances** – more than family circumstance, parents' educational background or income. It improves academic results, mental health, wealth, communication skills, ambition and happiness.[1]

The number of children reading for fun is in rapid decline. Young people have a lot of competition for their time. In 2024, 1 in 10 children and young people in the UK aged 5 to 18 did not own a single book at home.[2]

Hachette works extensively with schools, libraries and literacy charities, but here are some ways we can all raise more readers:

- Reading to children for just 10 minutes a day makes a difference
- Don't give up if children aren't regular readers – there will be books for them!
- Visit bookshops and libraries to get recommendations
- Encourage them to listen to audiobooks
- Support school libraries
- Give books as gifts

There's a lot more information about how to encourage children to read on our website: **www.RaisingReaders.co.uk**

Thank you for reading.

hachette
UK

---

[1] National Literacy Trust, Book Ownership in 2024, November 2024
https://nlt.cdn.ngo/media/documents/Book_ownership_in_2024

[2] OECD. 2021. 21st-century readers: developing literacy skills in a digital world. Paris, France: OECD Publishing.
https://www.oecd.org/en/publications/21st-century-readers_a83d84cb-en.html